To Learn More

AT THE LIBRARY

Hadithi, Mwenye. *Bumping Buffalo*. London, U.K.: Hodder Children's Division, 2010.

Stewart, Melissa. *Deadliest Animals*. Washington, D.C.: National Geographic, 2011.

Zobel, Derek. *Lions*. Minneapolis, Minn.: Bellwether Media, 2012.

ON THE WEB

Learning more about Cape buffalo is as easy as 1, 2, 3.

1. Go to www.factsurfer.com.

2. Enter "Cape buffalo" into the search box.

3. Click the "Surf" button and you will see a list of related web sites.

With factsurfer.com, finding more information is just a click away.

Index

The images in this book are reproduced through the courtesy of: BirdImages, front cover; smileimage9, p. 5; Martin Zwick/ agefotostock/ SuperStock, p. 7; Tier und Naturfotografie/ SuperStock, p. 9; Minden Pictures/ SuperStock, p. 11; Coastalmaps, p. 13; Tui De Roy/ Minden Pictures, p. 15; Panoramic Images/ Getty Images, p. 17 (top); Maggy Meyer, p. 17 (bottom left); Birdiegal, p. 17 (bottom right); Alta Oosthuizen, p. 19; Laurent Renaud/ Biosphoto, p. 21.

Cape Buffalo

by Megan Borgert-Spaniol

BELLWETHER MEDIA • MINNEAPOLIS, MN

Note to Librarians, Teachers, and Parents:

Blastoff! Readers are carefully developed by literacy experts and combine standards-based content with developmentally appropriate text.

Level 1 provides the most support through repetition of high-frequency words, light text, predictable sentence patterns, and strong visual support.

Level 2 offers early readers a bit more challenge through varied simple sentences, increased text load, and less repetition of high-frequency words.

Level 3 advances early-fluent readers toward fluency through increased text and concept load, less reliance on visuals, longer sentences, and more literary language.

Level 4 builds reading stamina by providing more text per page, increased use of punctuation, greater variation in sentence patterns, and increasingly challenging vocabulary.

Level 5 encourages children to move from "learning to read" to "reading to learn" by providing even more text, varied writing styles, and less familiar topics.

Whichever book is right for your reader, Blastoff! Readers are the perfect books to build confidence and encourage a love of reading that will last a lifetime!

This edition first published in 2014 by Bellwether Media, Inc.

No part of this publication may be reproduced in whole or in part without written permission of the publisher. For information regarding permission, write to Bellwether Media, Inc., Attention: Permissions Department, 5357 Penn Avenue South, Minneapolis, MN 55419.

Library of Congress Cataloging-in-Publication Data

Borgert-Spaniol, Megan, 1989- author.
  Cape Buffalo / by Megan Borgert-Spaniol.
    pages cm. – (Blastoff! Readers. Animal Safari)
  Summary: "Developed by literacy experts for students in kindergarten through grade three, this book introduces Cape buffalo to young readers through leveled text and related photos"– Provided by publisher.
  Audience: 5 to 8.
  Audience: K to grade 3.
  Includes bibliographical references and index.
  ISBN 978-1-60014-965-8 (hardcover : alk. paper)
  1. African buffalo–Juvenile literature. I. Title. II. Series: Blastoff! readers. 1, Animal safari.
  QL737.U53B678 2014
  599.64′2-dc23
                                                                    2014000111

Printed in the United States of America, North Mankato, MN.

Contents

What Are Cape Buffalo?

Cape buffalo are large **mammals**. They are known for their big horns.

A male's horns meet to form a **boss**. This protects his head in fights.

boss

Cape buffalo live in **savannahs**. They rest in the shade during the day.

They also roll in
mud to stay cool.
The mud protects
their skin from
the hot sun.

Herds

Cape buffalo travel in **herds**. They **graze** when the sun goes down.

13

Small birds follow
a herd. They eat
insects off
the buffalo.

Predators

A herd gathers at a **water hole** to drink. The buffalo keep watch for lions and other **predators**.

Lions look for
a slow or weak
buffalo. Then
they attack.

The herd charges
to protect the
buffalo. Back
off, lions!

Glossary

boss—a hard shield on the head of a male Cape buffalo

graze—to eat grasses and other plants on the ground

herds—groups of Cape buffalo that travel together

insects—small animals with six legs and hard outer bodies; insect bodies are divided into three parts.

mammals—warm-blooded animals that have backbones and feed their young milk

predators—animals that hunt other animals for food

savannahs—grasslands with scattered trees

water hole—a natural area filled with water; animals gather at water holes to drink.